50 Game Day Snack Recipes for Home

By: Kelly Johnson

Table of Contents

- Buffalo chicken wings
- Seven-layer dip
- Nachos with cheese and toppings
- BBQ pulled pork sliders
- Spinach and artichoke dip
- Mini meatballs in marinara sauce
- Guacamole with tortilla chips
- Chili con carne
- Jalapeno poppers
- Loaded potato skins
- Pigs in a blanket
- Queso dip
- Chicken tenders
- Deviled eggs
- Stuffed mushrooms
- Taco cups
- Onion rings
- Teriyaki chicken skewers
- Bruschetta
- Macaroni and cheese bites
- Caprese skewers
- Sausage rolls
- Baked spinach and feta dip
- Mini beef sliders
- Garlic breadsticks
- Vegetable spring rolls
- Crab cakes
- Smoked salmon crostini
- Mini pizza bites
- Cheese-stuffed jalapenos
- Chicken quesadillas
- Fried calamari
- Poutine
- Meatball sliders
- Chicken satay with peanut sauce

- Stuffed bell peppers
- Buffalo cauliflower bites
- Shrimp cocktail
- Teriyaki meatballs
- Sweet potato fries
- Cucumber rolls with cream cheese
- BBQ chicken drumsticks
- Bruschetta with tomato and basil
- Bacon-wrapped scallops
- Cornbread muffins
- Stuffed jalapeno poppers
- Philly cheesesteak sliders
- Mediterranean platter with hummus and pita
- Asian chicken wings
- Chocolate-covered strawberries

Buffalo chicken wings

Ingredients:

- 2-3 lbs chicken wings, split into flats and drumettes
- Salt and pepper, to taste
- 1 cup all-purpose flour
- 1 tsp paprika
- 1 tsp garlic powder
- Oil for frying (vegetable or canola oil)

For the Buffalo Sauce:

- 1/2 cup hot sauce (such as Frank's RedHot)
- 1/2 cup unsalted butter
- 1 tbsp honey (optional, for sweetness)
- 1 tsp Worcestershire sauce (optional, for extra depth)

Instructions:

1. Prepare the Chicken Wings:
    - Pat dry the chicken wings with paper towels. Season with salt and pepper.
2. Coat the Wings:
    - In a bowl, mix the flour, paprika, and garlic powder. Dredge each chicken wing piece in the flour mixture, shaking off excess.
3. Fry the Wings:
    - Heat oil in a deep fryer or large pot to 375°F (190°C). Fry the wings in batches for about 10-12 minutes, or until they are golden brown and crispy. Drain on paper towels.
4. Make the Buffalo Sauce:
    - In a saucepan, melt the butter over medium heat. Stir in the hot sauce (and honey and Worcestershire sauce if using) until well combined and heated through.
5. Coat the Wings in Sauce:
    - Toss the fried chicken wings in the buffalo sauce until evenly coated. For extra saucy wings, you can dip them back in the sauce or drizzle more over the top.
6. Serve:
    - Serve the buffalo wings hot with celery sticks and blue cheese or ranch dressing for dipping.

Enjoy your homemade buffalo chicken wings as a tasty treat for game day or any occasion!

Seven-layer dip

Ingredients:

- 1 can (16 oz) refried beans
- 1 packet (1 oz) taco seasoning mix
- 1 cup sour cream
- 1 cup guacamole (homemade or store-bought)
- 1 cup chunky salsa
- 1 cup shredded cheddar cheese (or Mexican blend cheese)
- 1/2 cup sliced black olives
- 1/2 cup diced tomatoes
- 1/4 cup chopped green onions
- Optional: chopped cilantro for garnish

Instructions:

1. Prepare the Refried Beans Layer:
    - In a small bowl, mix the refried beans with the taco seasoning until well combined.
2. Assemble the Layers:
    - Spread the refried beans evenly in the bottom of a 9x13 inch serving dish or a similarly sized platter.
    - Next, spread the sour cream evenly over the beans.
    - Follow with an even layer of guacamole.
    - Spread the salsa over the guacamole layer.
    - Sprinkle the shredded cheese evenly over the salsa.
    - Scatter the black olives over the cheese layer.
    - Top with diced tomatoes and chopped green onions.
3. Garnish and Serve:
    - If desired, garnish with chopped cilantro.
    - Serve immediately with tortilla chips for dipping.

Enjoy this delicious seven-layer dip as a crowd-pleasing appetizer at your next game day party or gathering!

Nachos with cheese and toppings

Ingredients:

- Tortilla chips (about 1 bag or enough to cover a baking sheet)
- 2 cups shredded cheddar cheese (or Mexican blend cheese)
- 1 can (15 oz) black beans, drained and rinsed
- 1 cup diced tomatoes
- 1/2 cup sliced black olives
- 1/2 cup sliced jalapenos (fresh or pickled)
- 1/4 cup chopped fresh cilantro
- 1/2 cup sour cream
- 1/4 cup salsa (optional, for extra flavor)
- Guacamole (optional, for serving)

Instructions:

1. Preheat the Oven:
   - Preheat your oven to 375°F (190°C).
2. Prepare the Baking Sheet:
   - Line a large baking sheet with parchment paper or foil for easy cleanup.
3. Assemble the Nachos:
   - Spread a single layer of tortilla chips on the prepared baking sheet.
   - Sprinkle half of the shredded cheese evenly over the chips.
   - Add half of the black beans, diced tomatoes, black olives, and jalapenos evenly over the cheese layer.
   - Sprinkle the remaining shredded cheese over the toppings.
4. Bake the Nachos:
   - Place the baking sheet in the preheated oven and bake for about 10-12 minutes, or until the cheese is melted and bubbly.
5. Add Fresh Toppings:
   - Remove the nachos from the oven and immediately sprinkle with chopped cilantro.
6. Serve:
   - Serve the nachos hot, with sour cream, salsa, and guacamole on the side for dipping.

Enjoy these delicious nachos with cheese and toppings as a satisfying snack during your game day festivities!

BBQ pulled pork sliders

Ingredients:

For the Pulled Pork:

- 2-3 lbs pork shoulder or pork butt
- Salt and pepper, to taste
- 1 cup BBQ sauce (plus extra for serving)
- 1 cup chicken broth or water
- 1 onion, chopped
- 3 cloves garlic, minced
- 1 tbsp olive oil

For the Sliders:

- Slider buns or mini hamburger buns
- Coleslaw (optional, for topping)
- Pickles (optional, for topping)

Instructions:

1. Prepare the Pork:
   - Season the pork shoulder with salt and pepper on all sides.
   - In a large skillet or Dutch oven, heat olive oil over medium-high heat. Sear the pork shoulder on all sides until browned, about 3-4 minutes per side.
2. Slow Cook the Pork:
   - Transfer the seared pork shoulder to a slow cooker.
   - Add chopped onion and minced garlic around the pork.
   - Pour in BBQ sauce and chicken broth (or water).
   - Cover and cook on low for 8-10 hours, or on high for 4-6 hours, until the pork is very tender and easily shreds with a fork.
3. Shred the Pork:
   - Remove the pork shoulder from the slow cooker and shred it using two forks. Discard any large pieces of fat.
4. Assemble the Sliders:
   - Split the slider buns or mini hamburger buns.
   - Place a generous amount of pulled pork onto the bottom half of each bun.
   - Drizzle extra BBQ sauce over the pulled pork if desired.
   - Top with coleslaw and pickles, if using.
5. Serve:
   - Close the sliders with the top half of the buns and secure with toothpicks, if needed.
   - Arrange the sliders on a serving platter and serve immediately.

These BBQ pulled pork sliders are sure to be a hit at your game day party or any casual gathering. Enjoy the delicious combination of tender pulled pork, tangy BBQ sauce, and crunchy coleslaw!

Spinach and artichoke dip

Ingredients:

- 1 (10 oz) package frozen chopped spinach, thawed and drained
- 1 (14 oz) can artichoke hearts, drained and chopped
- 1 cup grated Parmesan cheese
- 1 cup shredded mozzarella cheese
- 1 cup sour cream
- 1/2 cup mayonnaise
- 1/2 cup cream cheese, softened
- 2 cloves garlic, minced
- 1/2 tsp onion powder
- 1/2 tsp salt
- 1/4 tsp black pepper

Instructions:

1. Preheat the Oven:
    - Preheat your oven to 350°F (175°C).
2. Prepare the Spinach and Artichokes:
    - Ensure the frozen spinach is completely thawed. Squeeze out any excess water and chop it finely.
    - Drain and chop the artichoke hearts.
3. Mix the Ingredients:
    - In a large bowl, combine the chopped spinach, chopped artichoke hearts, grated Parmesan cheese, shredded mozzarella cheese, sour cream, mayonnaise, softened cream cheese, minced garlic, onion powder, salt, and black pepper. Mix until well combined.
4. Bake the Dip:
    - Transfer the mixture to a baking dish (such as an 8x8 inch dish or a similarly sized oven-safe dish).
    - Smooth the top with a spatula.
    - Bake in the preheated oven for 25-30 minutes, or until the dip is hot and bubbly, and the top is lightly golden brown.
5. Serve:
    - Remove from the oven and let it cool slightly before serving.
    - Serve the spinach and artichoke dip warm with tortilla chips, toasted bread slices, or vegetable sticks for dipping.

Enjoy this creamy and delicious spinach and artichoke dip as a delightful appetizer during your game day celebrations or any gathering!

Mini meatballs in marinara sauce

Ingredients:

For the Meatballs:

- 1 lb ground beef (or a mixture of beef and pork)
- 1/2 cup breadcrumbs
- 1/4 cup grated Parmesan cheese
- 1 egg
- 2 cloves garlic, minced
- 1/2 tsp salt
- 1/4 tsp black pepper
- 1/2 tsp dried oregano
- 1/2 tsp dried basil
- 1/4 cup chopped fresh parsley (optional, for garnish)

For the Marinara Sauce:

- 1 (24 oz) jar marinara sauce (or homemade marinara)
- 1 tbsp olive oil
- 1 onion, finely chopped
- 2 cloves garlic, minced
- 1/2 tsp dried oregano
- 1/2 tsp dried basil
- Salt and pepper, to taste

Instructions:

1. Make the Meatballs:
    - Preheat your oven to 400°F (200°C). Line a baking sheet with parchment paper or foil.
    - In a large bowl, combine the ground beef, breadcrumbs, grated Parmesan cheese, egg, minced garlic, salt, pepper, dried oregano, and dried basil. Mix until well combined.
    - Shape the mixture into small meatballs, about 1-inch in diameter, and place them on the prepared baking sheet.
    - Bake in the preheated oven for 12-15 minutes, or until the meatballs are cooked through and lightly browned.
2. Prepare the Marinara Sauce:
    - While the meatballs are baking, heat olive oil in a large skillet over medium heat.
    - Add the finely chopped onion and sauté until softened and translucent, about 3-4 minutes.
    - Stir in the minced garlic, dried oregano, and dried basil. Cook for another 1-2 minutes until fragrant.

- Pour in the marinara sauce and season with salt and pepper to taste. Stir well to combine.
- Reduce the heat to low and let the sauce simmer for 10-15 minutes, stirring occasionally.
3. Combine Meatballs and Sauce:
    - Once the meatballs are done baking, transfer them to the skillet with the marinara sauce.
    - Gently stir to coat the meatballs with the sauce.
    - Let them simmer together for another 5-10 minutes to allow the flavors to meld.
4. Serve:
    - Transfer the mini meatballs in marinara sauce to a serving dish.
    - Garnish with chopped fresh parsley if desired.
    - Serve hot with toothpicks for easy grabbing.

Enjoy these delicious mini meatballs in marinara sauce as a crowd-pleasing appetizer at your next game day party or gathering!

Guacamole with tortilla chips

Ingredients:

- 3 ripe avocados
- 1 lime, juiced
- 1/2 teaspoon salt, or to taste
- 1/2 teaspoon ground cumin
- 1/2 teaspoon cayenne pepper (optional, for spice)
- 1/2 cup diced red onion
- 1/2 cup diced tomato
- 1/4 cup chopped fresh cilantro
- 2 cloves garlic, minced
- Tortilla chips, for serving

Instructions:

1. Prepare the Avocados:
    - Cut the avocados in half, remove the pits, and scoop the flesh into a mixing bowl.
2. Mash the Avocados:
    - Mash the avocados with a fork or potato masher until smooth, or to your desired consistency (some prefer chunky guacamole).
3. Add Lime Juice and Seasonings:
    - Stir in the lime juice, salt, ground cumin, and cayenne pepper (if using). Mix well.
4. Add Vegetables and Herbs:
    - Gently fold in the diced red onion, diced tomato, chopped cilantro, and minced garlic. Mix until evenly distributed.
5. Adjust Seasonings:
    - Taste the guacamole and adjust salt, lime juice, or spices as needed to suit your preference.
6. Serve:
    - Transfer the guacamole to a serving bowl.
    - Serve with tortilla chips for dipping.

Enjoy your homemade guacamole with tortilla chips as a tasty and satisfying snack! Adjust the spice levels and ingredients to suit your taste preferences for a perfect game day treat.

Chili con carne

Ingredients:

- 1 lb ground beef (or ground turkey, chicken, or a combination)
- 1 onion, chopped
- 3 cloves garlic, minced
- 1 bell pepper (any color), chopped
- 1 can (14.5 oz) diced tomatoes
- 1 can (15 oz) kidney beans, drained and rinsed
- 1 can (15 oz) black beans, drained and rinsed
- 2 cups beef broth (or chicken broth)
- 2 tbsp tomato paste
- 2 tbsp chili powder
- 1 tsp ground cumin
- 1 tsp paprika
- 1/2 tsp dried oregano
- 1/2 tsp cayenne pepper (optional, for heat)
- Salt and pepper, to taste
- 1 tbsp olive oil
- Optional toppings: shredded cheese, sour cream, chopped cilantro, diced avocado

Instructions:

1. Brown the Meat:
   - Heat olive oil in a large pot or Dutch oven over medium-high heat. Add the ground beef and cook until browned, breaking it apart with a spoon as it cooks.
2. Saute Vegetables:
   - Add the chopped onion, minced garlic, and bell pepper to the pot. Cook, stirring occasionally, until the vegetables are softened, about 5-7 minutes.
3. Add Tomatoes and Beans:
   - Stir in the diced tomatoes (with their juices), drained and rinsed kidney beans, and drained and rinsed black beans.
4. Season the Chili:
   - Add the beef broth, tomato paste, chili powder, ground cumin, paprika, dried oregano, cayenne pepper (if using), salt, and pepper. Stir well to combine.
5. Simmer:
   - Bring the chili to a boil, then reduce the heat to low. Cover and simmer for 30-45 minutes, stirring occasionally, until the flavors have melded and the chili has thickened to your desired consistency.
6. Serve:
   - Ladle the chili into bowls.
   - Serve hot, topped with shredded cheese, a dollop of sour cream, chopped cilantro, and diced avocado if desired.

Enjoy this hearty and comforting chili con carne with your favorite toppings, alongside cornbread or tortilla chips for a delicious game day meal!

Jalapeno poppers

Ingredients:

- 12 fresh jalapeno peppers
- 8 oz cream cheese, softened
- 1 cup shredded cheddar cheese (or Mexican blend cheese)
- 1/2 teaspoon garlic powder
- 1/2 teaspoon onion powder
- 1/4 teaspoon paprika
- Salt and pepper, to taste
- 1 cup breadcrumbs
- 2 eggs, beaten
- Oil for frying (optional) or cooking spray

Instructions:

1. Prepare the Jalapenos:
    - Preheat your oven to 375°F (190°C).
    - Slice each jalapeno pepper in half lengthwise. Use a spoon to scoop out the seeds and membranes, creating a cavity for the filling. (Wear gloves to protect your hands from the jalapeno juices.)
2. Make the Filling:
    - In a mixing bowl, combine the softened cream cheese, shredded cheddar cheese, garlic powder, onion powder, paprika, salt, and pepper. Mix until smooth and well combined.
3. Fill the Jalapeno Halves:
    - Spoon the cheese mixture into each jalapeno half, filling them generously.
4. Coat the Jalapeno Poppers:
    - Place the breadcrumbs in a shallow dish.
    - Dip each filled jalapeno half into the beaten eggs, then roll it in the breadcrumbs, coating evenly.
5. Bake or Fry the Jalapeno Poppers:
    - Bake Option: Arrange the coated jalapeno poppers on a baking sheet lined with parchment paper. Bake in the preheated oven for 20-25 minutes, or until the jalapenos are tender and the filling is hot and bubbly.
    - Fry Option (optional for a crispier texture): Heat oil in a deep fryer or large skillet to 350°F (175°C). Fry the coated jalapeno poppers in batches for about 2-3 minutes per side, or until golden brown. Drain on paper towels.
6. Serve:
    - Serve the jalapeno poppers hot as they are or with a dipping sauce like ranch dressing, salsa, or sour cream.

Enjoy these delicious homemade jalapeno poppers as a spicy and creamy appetizer for your game day festivities or any occasion!

Loaded potato skins

Ingredients:

- 4 large baking potatoes (such as russet)
- 2 tbsp olive oil
- Salt and pepper, to taste
- 1 cup shredded cheddar cheese (or Mexican blend cheese)
- 4 slices bacon, cooked and crumbled
- 2 green onions, thinly sliced
- 1/2 cup sour cream
- Optional: chopped fresh parsley or chives for garnish

Instructions:

1. Preheat the Oven:
   - Preheat your oven to 400°F (200°C).
2. Prepare the Potatoes:
   - Scrub the potatoes clean and pat them dry with paper towels.
   - Pierce each potato several times with a fork to allow steam to escape during baking.
3. Bake the Potatoes:
   - Rub each potato with olive oil and sprinkle with salt and pepper.
   - Place the potatoes directly on the oven rack or on a baking sheet lined with foil.
   - Bake for 45-60 minutes, or until the potatoes are tender when pierced with a fork.
4. Prepare the Potato Skins:
   - Remove the potatoes from the oven and let them cool slightly until they are safe to handle.
   - Slice each potato in half lengthwise. Carefully scoop out the flesh, leaving about 1/4 inch of potato attached to the skin (save the scooped-out potato flesh for another use, like mashed potatoes).
5. Add Toppings:
   - Arrange the potato skins on a baking sheet, skin-side down.
   - Sprinkle shredded cheddar cheese evenly inside each potato skin.
   - Top with crumbled bacon and sliced green onions.
6. Bake Again:
   - Return the loaded potato skins to the oven and bake for an additional 10-15 minutes, or until the cheese is melted and bubbly.
7. Serve:
   - Remove from the oven and let cool slightly.
   - Top each loaded potato skin with a dollop of sour cream.
   - Garnish with chopped fresh parsley or chives if desired.

Enjoy these delicious loaded potato skins as a satisfying appetizer or snack during your game day celebrations or any casual gathering!

Pigs in a blanket

Ingredients:

- 1 can (8 oz) refrigerated crescent roll dough (8 count)
- 32 cocktail sausages (mini hot dogs)
- Mustard or ketchup, for serving (optional)

Instructions:

1. Preheat the Oven:
   - Preheat your oven to 375°F (190°C).
2. Prepare the Dough:
   - Open the can of crescent roll dough and separate it into triangles along the perforated lines.
3. Wrap the Sausages:
   - Take each mini sausage and wrap it in one triangle of crescent roll dough. Start from the wide end of the triangle and roll it up to the point, enclosing the sausage completely.
4. Arrange on Baking Sheet:
   - Place the wrapped sausages seam-side down on a baking sheet lined with parchment paper or lightly greased.
5. Bake:
   - Bake in the preheated oven for 12-15 minutes, or until the crescent roll dough is golden brown and cooked through.
6. Serve:
   - Remove from the oven and let cool slightly before serving.
   - Serve pigs in a blanket warm with mustard or ketchup for dipping.

Enjoy these delightful pigs in a blanket as a tasty and nostalgic appetizer at your next game day gathering or party!

Queso dip

Ingredients:

- 8 oz (about 2 cups) shredded cheese (such as cheddar, Monterey Jack, or a blend)
- 1 tbsp cornstarch
- 1 cup whole milk or half-and-half
- 1 can (10 oz) diced tomatoes with green chilies (like Rotel), undrained
- 1/2 tsp ground cumin
- 1/2 tsp chili powder
- Salt and pepper, to taste
- Optional: chopped fresh cilantro, diced jalapenos, or hot sauce for extra heat

Instructions:

1. Prepare the Cheese Mixture:
    - In a bowl, toss the shredded cheese with cornstarch until evenly coated. This helps thicken the queso.
2. Heat the Milk:
    - In a saucepan over medium heat, warm the whole milk or half-and-half until just simmering.
3. Add Cheese and Seasonings:
    - Reduce the heat to low. Gradually add the cheese mixture, stirring constantly until the cheese is melted and the mixture is smooth.
4. Add Tomatoes and Seasonings:
    - Stir in the diced tomatoes with green chilies (undrained), ground cumin, chili powder, salt, and pepper. Continue to cook, stirring occasionally, for another 2-3 minutes until heated through and flavors are blended.
5. Adjust Consistency:
    - If the queso dip is too thick, you can thin it out with a bit more milk. If it's too thin, continue to cook for a few more minutes until it reaches the desired consistency.
6. Serve:
    - Transfer the queso dip to a serving bowl or a warm slow cooker to keep it warm.
    - Optionally, garnish with chopped fresh cilantro, diced jalapenos, or a dash of hot sauce for extra flavor.
7. Enjoy:
    - Serve the queso dip warm with tortilla chips, vegetable sticks, or your favorite snacks for dipping.

This homemade queso dip is sure to be a hit at your game day party or any gathering. Adjust the level of spiciness by choosing mild or hot diced tomatoes with green chilies and adding jalapenos or hot sauce to taste.

Chicken tenders

Ingredients:

- 1 lb chicken tenderloins (or chicken breasts, cut into strips)
- 1 cup buttermilk (or regular milk)
- 1 tsp garlic powder
- 1 tsp paprika
- 1/2 tsp salt
- 1/4 tsp black pepper
- 1 cup all-purpose flour
- 1 cup breadcrumbs (panko breadcrumbs work well for extra crunch)
- 1/2 cup grated Parmesan cheese (optional, for extra flavor)
- Vegetable oil, for frying (about 2 cups, or enough for shallow frying)

Instructions:

1. Prepare the Chicken:
    - In a bowl, combine the buttermilk (or regular milk), garlic powder, paprika, salt, and black pepper. Mix well.
    - Add the chicken tenderloins to the buttermilk mixture, ensuring they are fully coated. Cover the bowl and refrigerate for at least 30 minutes (or up to 4 hours) to marinate.
2. Prepare the Breading Station:
    - In one shallow dish, place the flour.
    - In another shallow dish, combine the breadcrumbs and grated Parmesan cheese (if using).
3. Bread the Chicken:
    - Remove each piece of chicken from the buttermilk marinade, allowing any excess liquid to drip off.
    - Dredge each chicken tender in the flour, shaking off any excess.
    - Dip the floured chicken tender back into the buttermilk mixture, ensuring it's coated.
    - Finally, coat the chicken tender in the breadcrumb mixture, pressing gently to adhere the breadcrumbs to all sides. Place the breaded chicken on a plate or wire rack.
4. Fry the Chicken Tenders:
    - Heat vegetable oil in a large skillet over medium-high heat, about 1/2 inch deep.
    - Once the oil is hot (around 350°F or 175°C), carefully add the chicken tenders in batches, making sure not to overcrowd the pan.
    - Fry the chicken tenders for 3-4 minutes per side, or until golden brown and cooked through. The internal temperature should reach 165°F (75°C).
    - Remove the cooked chicken tenders from the oil and drain on a plate lined with paper towels.

5. Serve:
    - Serve the crispy chicken tenders hot with your favorite dipping sauces, such as barbecue sauce, honey mustard, or ranch dressing.

Enjoy these homemade chicken tenders as a delicious snack or main dish during your game day festivities or any mealtime!

Deviled eggs

Ingredients:

- 6 large eggs
- 1/4 cup mayonnaise
- 1 tsp Dijon mustard
- 1/2 tsp white vinegar
- Salt and pepper, to taste
- Paprika, for garnish
- Optional: chopped fresh chives or parsley for garnish

Instructions:

1. Hard-boil the Eggs:
    - Place the eggs in a single layer in a saucepan and cover with water.
    - Bring the water to a boil over medium-high heat.
    - Once boiling, remove the pan from heat, cover, and let the eggs sit in the hot water for 10-12 minutes.
2. Cool and Peel the Eggs:
    - Drain the hot water from the saucepan and run cold water over the eggs until they are cool enough to handle.
    - Gently tap each egg on a hard surface to crack the shell, then peel under cold running water.
3. Prepare the Filling:
    - Slice each egg in half lengthwise. Carefully remove the yolks and place them in a small bowl.
    - Mash the egg yolks with a fork until smooth.
4. Make the Deviled Egg Filling:
    - To the mashed yolks, add mayonnaise, Dijon mustard, white vinegar, salt, and pepper. Mix until well combined and creamy.
5. Fill the Egg Whites:
    - Spoon or pipe the yolk mixture evenly into the hollows of the egg whites.
6. Garnish and Serve:
    - Sprinkle the deviled eggs with paprika for color and optional chopped fresh chives or parsley for added flavor.
7. Chill and Serve:
    - Refrigerate the deviled eggs for at least 30 minutes to allow the flavors to meld.
    - Serve cold as a delightful appetizer or side dish.

Deviled eggs are versatile, and you can customize them by adding ingredients like diced pickles, relish, or a dash of hot sauce to the filling. Enjoy these classic deviled eggs at your next gathering or game day party!

Stuffed mushrooms

Ingredients:

- 24 large white or cremini mushrooms
- 1/2 cup Italian-style breadcrumbs
- 1/4 cup grated Parmesan cheese
- 2 cloves garlic, minced
- 2 tbsp chopped fresh parsley
- 1/4 cup olive oil
- Salt and pepper, to taste
- Optional: 1/4 cup chopped sun-dried tomatoes, 1/4 cup chopped cooked bacon, or 1/4 cup chopped spinach

Instructions:

1. Prepare the Mushrooms:
    - Preheat your oven to 375°F (190°C).
    - Clean the mushrooms with a damp paper towel to remove any dirt. Remove the stems from the mushrooms and finely chop them. Set the mushroom caps aside.
2. Prepare the Filling:
    - In a bowl, combine the chopped mushroom stems, Italian-style breadcrumbs, grated Parmesan cheese, minced garlic, chopped fresh parsley, and olive oil. Mix well to combine.
    - Season with salt and pepper to taste. Optionally, you can add chopped sun-dried tomatoes, cooked bacon, or spinach for additional flavor.
3. Stuff the Mushrooms:
    - Place the mushroom caps on a baking sheet, cavity side up.
    - Spoon the breadcrumb mixture evenly into each mushroom cap, pressing lightly to pack the filling.
4. Bake the Stuffed Mushrooms:
    - Bake in the preheated oven for 18-20 minutes, or until the mushrooms are tender and the filling is golden brown.
5. Serve:
    - Remove from the oven and let cool slightly before serving.
    - Arrange the stuffed mushrooms on a platter and serve warm.

These stuffed mushrooms are flavorful and versatile. They make a great appetizer for entertaining guests or as a tasty snack for game day. Enjoy!

Taco cups

Ingredients:

- 24 wonton wrappers
- 1 lb ground beef (or ground turkey)
- 1 packet (1 oz) taco seasoning mix
- 1/2 cup water
- 1 cup shredded cheddar cheese (or Mexican blend cheese)
- 1 cup salsa
- Optional toppings: diced tomatoes, chopped lettuce, sour cream, sliced olives, diced avocado

Instructions:

1. Preheat the Oven:
    - Preheat your oven to 375°F (190°C).
2. Prepare the Wonton Cups:
    - Lightly grease a 12-cup muffin tin.
    - Press one wonton wrapper into each muffin cup, gently pressing down and shaping it to form a cup shape.
3. Cook the Taco Meat:
    - In a skillet over medium heat, cook the ground beef until browned and cooked through.
    - Drain any excess grease from the skillet.
    - Stir in the taco seasoning mix and water. Simmer for 5 minutes, stirring occasionally, until the mixture has thickened slightly.
4. Assemble the Taco Cups:
    - Spoon a tablespoon of the taco meat mixture into each wonton cup.
    - Top each cup with a tablespoon of shredded cheese.
5. Bake the Taco Cups:
    - Bake in the preheated oven for 10-12 minutes, or until the wonton wrappers are golden brown and the cheese is melted and bubbly.
6. Serve:
    - Remove the taco cups from the muffin tin and arrange them on a serving platter.
    - Top each taco cup with salsa and your favorite toppings such as diced tomatoes, chopped lettuce, sour cream, sliced olives, and diced avocado.

Enjoy these delicious taco cups as a crowd-pleasing appetizer or snack at your next game day party or gathering!

Onion rings

Ingredients:

- 2 large onions (such as yellow or sweet onions)
- 1 cup all-purpose flour
- 1 tsp baking powder
- 1/2 tsp salt
- 1/2 tsp paprika
- 1/4 tsp black pepper
- 1 cup buttermilk (or regular milk)
- Vegetable oil, for frying
- Optional: additional seasoning like garlic powder, cayenne pepper, or smoked paprika

Instructions:

1. Prepare the Onions:
    - Peel the onions and cut them into 1/2-inch thick slices. Separate the slices into rings and discard the smallest inner rings or save them for another use.
2. Prepare the Batter:
    - In a large bowl, whisk together the flour, baking powder, salt, paprika, black pepper, and any optional additional seasonings you prefer.
3. Coat the Onion Rings:
    - Pour the buttermilk into a separate shallow bowl.
    - Dip each onion ring into the flour mixture, coating evenly, then dip it into the buttermilk, and finally dip it back into the flour mixture, ensuring it is well coated. Shake off any excess flour.
4. Fry the Onion Rings:
    - In a large, deep skillet or Dutch oven, heat vegetable oil to 375°F (190°C).
    - Carefully place the coated onion rings into the hot oil in batches, making sure not to overcrowd the pan.
    - Fry the onion rings for 2-3 minutes per side, or until golden brown and crispy.
    - Remove the fried onion rings from the oil using a slotted spoon or tongs and transfer them to a plate lined with paper towels to drain excess oil.
5. Serve:
    - Serve the crispy onion rings hot as a side dish or snack.
    - Optionally, sprinkle with additional salt or your favorite seasoning before serving.

Enjoy these homemade crispy onion rings as a delicious and satisfying treat at your next meal or gathering!

Teriyaki chicken skewers

Ingredients:

- 1 lb boneless, skinless chicken thighs or chicken breast, cut into 1-inch cubes
- Bamboo skewers, soaked in water for 30 minutes (to prevent burning)
- Sesame seeds and chopped green onions, for garnish (optional)

For the Teriyaki Marinade:

- 1/2 cup soy sauce (use low sodium if preferred)
- 1/4 cup water
- 2 tbsp rice vinegar
- 2 tbsp honey or brown sugar
- 2 cloves garlic, minced
- 1 tsp grated ginger (or 1/2 tsp ground ginger)
- 1 tbsp cornstarch
- 1 tbsp water

Instructions:

1. Prepare the Teriyaki Marinade:
   - In a small saucepan, combine soy sauce, water, rice vinegar, honey or brown sugar, minced garlic, and grated ginger.
   - Bring the mixture to a simmer over medium heat, stirring occasionally.
2. Thicken the Sauce:
   - In a small bowl, mix cornstarch with 1 tablespoon of water until smooth.
   - Slowly pour the cornstarch slurry into the simmering sauce, stirring constantly until the sauce thickens. Remove from heat and let it cool slightly.
3. Marinate the Chicken:
   - Place the chicken cubes in a bowl or resealable plastic bag.
   - Pour half of the teriyaki marinade over the chicken, reserving the other half for basting and serving later.
   - Marinate the chicken in the refrigerator for at least 30 minutes, or up to 2 hours for more flavor.
4. Skewer the Chicken:
   - Preheat your grill to medium-high heat or preheat your oven to 400°F (200°C).
   - Thread the marinated chicken cubes onto the soaked bamboo skewers, dividing evenly.
5. Grill or Bake the Skewers:
   - Grilling: Place the skewers on the preheated grill. Grill for 5-7 minutes per side, or until the chicken is cooked through and has nice grill marks. Baste with reserved teriyaki sauce while grilling.

- Baking: Arrange the skewers on a baking sheet lined with parchment paper. Bake in the preheated oven for 15-20 minutes, or until the chicken is cooked through, turning once and basting with reserved teriyaki sauce halfway through.
6. Serve:
    - Remove the teriyaki chicken skewers from the grill or oven.
    - Brush with any remaining teriyaki sauce and sprinkle with sesame seeds and chopped green onions for garnish if desired.
    - Serve hot with steamed rice and vegetables, or as a delicious appetizer for your game day feast.

Enjoy these flavorful teriyaki chicken skewers as a tasty addition to your game day menu or any meal!

Bruschetta

Ingredients:

- 1 French baguette or Italian loaf, sliced into 1/2 inch thick slices
- 4-5 ripe tomatoes, diced
- 2 cloves garlic, minced
- 1/4 cup fresh basil leaves, chopped
- 2 tbsp extra virgin olive oil
- 1 tbsp balsamic vinegar (optional)
- Salt and freshly ground black pepper, to taste

Instructions:

1. Prepare the Bread:
   - Preheat the oven to 400°F (200°C).
   - Arrange the bread slices on a baking sheet. You can brush them lightly with olive oil if desired for extra flavor.
2. Toast the Bread:
   - Toast the bread slices in the preheated oven for about 5-7 minutes, or until they are lightly golden and crispy. Remove from the oven and let them cool slightly.
3. Prepare the Bruschetta Topping:
   - In a mixing bowl, combine the diced tomatoes, minced garlic, chopped basil, olive oil, and balsamic vinegar (if using).
   - Season with salt and pepper to taste. Mix well to combine all the flavors.
4. Assemble the Bruschetta:
   - Spoon the tomato mixture generously onto each toasted bread slice.
5. Serve:
   - Arrange the bruschetta on a serving platter.
   - Optionally, garnish with additional chopped basil leaves or a drizzle of balsamic glaze for presentation.
6. Enjoy:
   - Serve the bruschetta immediately as a flavorful appetizer or snack.

Bruschetta is best enjoyed fresh, so assemble it just before serving to maintain the crispy texture of the bread and the vibrant flavors of the tomatoes and basil. It's a perfect addition to your game day spread or any gathering!

Macaroni and cheese bites

Ingredients:

- 1 1/2 cups elbow macaroni (about 6 oz)
- 2 tbsp unsalted butter
- 2 tbsp all-purpose flour
- 1 cup milk
- 1 1/2 cups shredded cheddar cheese (or a blend of cheeses)
- 1/2 cup grated Parmesan cheese
- 1/2 tsp salt, or to taste
- 1/4 tsp black pepper
- 1/4 tsp garlic powder
- 1/4 tsp onion powder
- 1/4 cup breadcrumbs
- 1/4 cup grated Parmesan cheese (for coating)
- 2 eggs, beaten
- Vegetable oil, for frying

Instructions:

1. Cook the Macaroni:
    - Cook the elbow macaroni according to package instructions until al dente. Drain and set aside.
2. Make the Cheese Sauce:
    - In a saucepan, melt the butter over medium heat.
    - Stir in the flour and cook for about 1 minute, stirring constantly, to make a roux.
    - Gradually whisk in the milk, stirring constantly until the mixture thickens and comes to a simmer.
    - Reduce the heat to low and stir in the shredded cheddar cheese and grated Parmesan cheese until melted and smooth.
    - Season with salt, pepper, garlic powder, and onion powder. Remove from heat.
3. Combine Macaroni and Cheese Sauce:
    - Add the cooked macaroni to the cheese sauce and stir until well combined. Let the mixture cool slightly.
4. Form the Macaroni and Cheese Bites:
    - Line a baking sheet with parchment paper.
    - Scoop tablespoon-sized portions of the macaroni and cheese mixture and roll them into balls using your hands. Place the balls on the baking sheet.
5. Coat the Bites:
    - In a shallow bowl, combine the breadcrumbs and grated Parmesan cheese.
    - Dip each macaroni and cheese ball first into the beaten eggs, then roll them in the breadcrumb mixture until evenly coated. Place them back on the baking sheet.

6. Fry the Bites:
    - In a large skillet or pot, heat vegetable oil over medium heat until it reaches 350°F (175°C).
    - Carefully add the coated macaroni and cheese bites to the hot oil in batches, making sure not to overcrowd the pan.
    - Fry for about 2-3 minutes per batch, turning occasionally, until golden brown and crispy.
    - Remove the bites from the oil using a slotted spoon and place them on a plate lined with paper towels to drain excess oil.
7. Serve:
    - Let the macaroni and cheese bites cool slightly before serving.
    - Serve warm as a delicious appetizer or snack, optionally with marinara sauce or ranch dressing for dipping.

These crispy and creamy macaroni and cheese bites are sure to be a hit at your next game day party or gathering. Enjoy!

Caprese skewers

Ingredients:

- Fresh mozzarella balls (bocconcini), about 24 pieces
- Cherry tomatoes, about 24 pieces
- Fresh basil leaves, about 24 leaves
- Balsamic glaze, for drizzling (optional)
- Extra virgin olive oil, for drizzling
- Salt and pepper, to taste
- Wooden skewers or toothpicks

Instructions:

1. Prepare the Ingredients:
    - If using wooden skewers, soak them in water for about 30 minutes to prevent burning.
2. Assemble the Skewers:
    - On each skewer or toothpick, thread one cherry tomato, one basil leaf (folded if large), and one mozzarella ball. Repeat to make as many skewers as desired.
3. Drizzle and Season:
    - Arrange the Caprese skewers on a serving platter.
    - Drizzle with balsamic glaze and extra virgin olive oil.
    - Season lightly with salt and pepper, if desired.
4. Serve:
    - Serve the Caprese skewers immediately as a fresh and flavorful appetizer.

Caprese skewers are not only delicious but also visually appealing, making them a perfect addition to any party or gathering. Enjoy these bite-sized treats showcasing the wonderful combination of mozzarella, tomatoes, and basil!

Sausage rolls

Ingredients:

- 1 sheet of puff pastry (store-bought, thawed if frozen)
- 8 pork sausages (or any preferred sausage)
- 1 egg, beaten (for egg wash)
- Sesame seeds or poppy seeds (optional, for topping)

Instructions:

1. Preheat the Oven:
   - Preheat your oven to 400°F (200°C) and line a baking sheet with parchment paper.
2. Prepare the Sausages:
   - Remove the sausage meat from the casings, if using sausages with casings. Alternatively, use pre-ground sausage meat.
   - Divide each sausage into two portions (or as needed to fit the length of your puff pastry).
3. Prepare the Puff Pastry:
   - Roll out the puff pastry on a lightly floured surface into a rectangle approximately 12x10 inches (30x25 cm).
   - Cut the pastry lengthwise into two equal strips.
4. Assemble the Sausage Rolls:
   - Place a line of sausage meat along the length of each pastry strip, leaving a small border along one edge.
   - Roll the pastry over the sausage meat, sealing the edge with a bit of water or beaten egg.
   - Repeat with the second pastry strip and remaining sausage meat.
5. Cut and Glaze:
   - Cut each long roll into smaller pieces, about 2 inches (5 cm) in length.
   - Place the sausage rolls seam-side down on the prepared baking sheet.
   - Brush the tops of the sausage rolls with beaten egg and sprinkle with sesame seeds or poppy seeds, if desired.
6. Bake:
   - Bake in the preheated oven for 20-25 minutes, or until the pastry is golden brown and cooked through.
7. Serve:
   - Remove from the oven and let cool slightly on a wire rack.
   - Serve warm as a delicious snack or party food.

These homemade sausage rolls are versatile and can be customized by adding herbs or spices to the sausage meat, or by serving with dipping sauces like mustard or ketchup. Enjoy them fresh from the oven at your next gathering or game day party!

Baked spinach and feta dip

Ingredients:

- 8 oz (about 1 cup) frozen chopped spinach, thawed and drained
- 8 oz cream cheese, softened
- 1/2 cup sour cream
- 1/2 cup mayonnaise
- 1 cup crumbled feta cheese
- 1/2 cup grated Parmesan cheese
- 2 cloves garlic, minced
- 1/2 tsp onion powder
- 1/2 tsp dried dill (optional)
- Salt and pepper, to taste
- Optional: chopped green onions or parsley for garnish

Instructions:

1. Preheat the Oven:
    - Preheat your oven to 350°F (175°C).
2. Prepare the Spinach:
    - Thaw the frozen chopped spinach and drain well to remove excess moisture. You can squeeze it with your hands or press it with a paper towel.
3. Mix the Ingredients:
    - In a large bowl, combine the softened cream cheese, sour cream, mayonnaise, crumbled feta cheese, grated Parmesan cheese, minced garlic, onion powder, dried dill (if using), salt, and pepper. Mix until well combined.
    - Stir in the drained spinach until evenly distributed.
4. Bake the Dip:
    - Transfer the mixture to a baking dish or oven-safe skillet, spreading it out evenly.
5. Bake:
    - Bake in the preheated oven for 25-30 minutes, or until the dip is bubbly and lightly golden brown on top.
6. Serve:
    - Remove from the oven and let the dip cool slightly.
    - Garnish with chopped green onions or parsley, if desired.
    - Serve warm with tortilla chips, bread slices, or vegetable sticks for dipping.

This baked spinach and feta dip is creamy, cheesy, and packed with flavor. It's sure to be a crowd-pleaser at any gathering or party! Enjoy the delicious combination of spinach and feta in every bite.

Mini beef sliders

Ingredients:

- 1 lb ground beef (preferably 80% lean)
- Salt and pepper, to taste
- 1/2 tsp garlic powder
- 1/2 tsp onion powder
- 1/2 cup finely chopped onion
- 1/4 cup breadcrumbs
- 1 egg
- 12 slider buns
- Cheese slices (optional)
- Lettuce leaves, tomato slices, pickles, or any preferred toppings
- Ketchup, mustard, mayonnaise, or other condiments

Instructions:

1. Prepare the Beef Patties:
    - In a large bowl, combine the ground beef, salt, pepper, garlic powder, onion powder, finely chopped onion, breadcrumbs, and egg.
    - Mix gently until all ingredients are well combined, but do not overmix as it can toughen the meat.
2. Form the Patties:
    - Divide the beef mixture into 12 equal portions.
    - Shape each portion into small patties, slightly larger than the slider buns as they will shrink slightly when cooked.
3. Cook the Patties:
    - Heat a grill pan, skillet, or grill over medium-high heat.
    - Cook the patties for 3-4 minutes per side, or until they reach your desired level of doneness.
    - If adding cheese, place a slice of cheese on each patty during the last minute of cooking and cover with a lid to melt.
4. Assemble the Sliders:
    - Slice the slider buns in half horizontally.
    - Place a beef patty on the bottom half of each bun.
    - Add your preferred toppings such as lettuce, tomato slices, pickles, etc.
5. Serve:
    - Close the sliders with the top half of the buns.
    - Secure each slider with a toothpick if needed.
    - Serve warm with condiments like ketchup, mustard, or mayonnaise on the side.

These mini beef sliders are perfect for serving a crowd and can be customized with various toppings to suit everyone's tastes. They're sure to be a hit at your next game day party or gathering!

Garlic breadsticks

Ingredients:

- 1 lb (about 3 1/4 cups) all-purpose flour
- 1 tbsp sugar
- 1 tsp salt
- 2 1/4 tsp instant yeast (or one packet)
- 1 cup warm water (about 110°F)
- 3 tbsp olive oil
- 4 cloves garlic, minced
- 1/4 cup unsalted butter, melted
- 1/2 tsp garlic powder
- 1/2 tsp dried oregano
- 1/4 cup grated Parmesan cheese
- Salt, to taste
- Optional: additional grated Parmesan cheese and chopped parsley for garnish

Instructions:

1. Prepare the Dough:
    - In a large bowl, combine the flour, sugar, salt, and instant yeast.
    - Add the warm water and olive oil to the dry ingredients. Mix until a dough forms.
    - Turn the dough out onto a lightly floured surface and knead for about 5-7 minutes, or until smooth and elastic.
2. First Rise:
    - Place the dough in a lightly oiled bowl and cover with a clean kitchen towel or plastic wrap.
    - Let the dough rise in a warm, draft-free place for about 1 hour, or until doubled in size.
3. Shape the Breadsticks:
    - Preheat your oven to 400°F (200°C). Line a baking sheet with parchment paper.
    - Punch down the risen dough and divide it into 12 equal portions.
    - Roll each portion into a rope about 8-10 inches long and place them on the prepared baking sheet, leaving space between each breadstick.
4. Prepare the Garlic Butter Topping:
    - In a small bowl, combine the melted butter, minced garlic, garlic powder, dried oregano, grated Parmesan cheese, and salt to taste.
    - Mix well to combine.
5. Bake the Breadsticks:
    - Brush the garlic butter mixture generously over each breadstick, ensuring it's evenly coated.
    - Bake in the preheated oven for 12-15 minutes, or until the breadsticks are golden brown and cooked through.

6. Serve:
    - Remove from the oven and let the breadsticks cool slightly on a wire rack.
    - Optionally, sprinkle with additional grated Parmesan cheese and chopped parsley for garnish.
    - Serve warm as a delicious side dish or snack.

These homemade garlic breadsticks are soft on the inside, crispy on the outside, and packed with savory garlic and Parmesan flavors. They're perfect for sharing with family and friends at any meal!

Vegetable spring rolls

Ingredients:

- 10-12 spring roll wrappers (also known as rice paper wrappers)
- 2 cups shredded cabbage (green or purple)
- 1 cup shredded carrots
- 1 cup bean sprouts
- 1 cup thinly sliced bell peppers (red, yellow, or orange)
- 1/2 cup chopped green onions
- 1/4 cup chopped fresh cilantro or Thai basil (optional)
- 2 cloves garlic, minced
- 1 tbsp soy sauce
- 1 tbsp oyster sauce (optional)
- 1 tbsp sesame oil
- 1 tsp grated ginger
- 1 tsp sugar
- 1/2 tsp salt
- 1/4 tsp black pepper
- Vegetable oil, for frying
- Sweet chili sauce or soy sauce, for dipping

Instructions:

1. Prepare the Filling:
    - In a large bowl, combine shredded cabbage, shredded carrots, bean sprouts, sliced bell peppers, green onions, and chopped cilantro or Thai basil (if using).
2. Make the Sauce:
    - In a small bowl, whisk together minced garlic, soy sauce, oyster sauce (if using), sesame oil, grated ginger, sugar, salt, and black pepper.
3. Cook the Filling:
    - Heat a large skillet or wok over medium-high heat.
    - Add the sauce mixture to the skillet and stir-fry for 2-3 minutes, until the vegetables are slightly softened but still crisp.
    - Remove from heat and let the filling cool slightly.
4. Assemble the Spring Rolls:
    - Prepare a clean, damp kitchen towel on your work surface.
    - Fill a shallow dish with warm water.
    - Dip one spring roll wrapper into the warm water for a few seconds until it softens.
    - Lay the wrapper flat on the damp towel.
5. Add the Filling:
    - Place a spoonful of the vegetable filling along the bottom edge of the wrapper, leaving space on the sides.

- Fold the bottom edge of the wrapper over the filling, then fold in the sides, and roll tightly to enclose the filling. Repeat with remaining wrappers and filling.
6. Fry the Spring Rolls:
    - In a large skillet or pot, heat vegetable oil over medium heat to 350°F (175°C).
    - Carefully add a few spring rolls at a time, seam side down, and fry for 2-3 minutes per side, or until golden brown and crispy.
    - Use tongs to remove the spring rolls from the oil and place them on a plate lined with paper towels to drain excess oil.
7. Serve:
    - Serve the vegetable spring rolls hot with sweet chili sauce or soy sauce for dipping.

These homemade vegetable spring rolls are crunchy on the outside and filled with flavorful vegetables on the inside. They make a delicious appetizer or snack for any occasion!

Crab cakes

Ingredients:

- 1 lb lump crab meat, picked over for shells
- 1/3 cup mayonnaise
- 1 large egg
- 1 tbsp Dijon mustard
- 1 tbsp Worcestershire sauce
- 1/4 cup chopped green onions (scallions)
- 1/4 cup chopped fresh parsley
- 1/2 cup breadcrumbs (plus extra for coating)
- Salt and pepper, to taste
- 1/4 tsp Old Bay seasoning (optional)
- 1/4 cup vegetable oil, for frying
- Lemon wedges, for serving

Instructions:

1. **Prepare the Crab Cakes:**
    - In a large bowl, gently combine the lump crab meat, mayonnaise, egg, Dijon mustard, Worcestershire sauce, green onions, parsley, breadcrumbs, salt, pepper, and Old Bay seasoning (if using). Be careful not to break up the crab meat too much.
2. **Form the Crab Cakes:**
    - Divide the mixture into 8 equal portions.
    - Shape each portion into a round patty about 1 inch thick.
    - Place the crab cakes on a baking sheet lined with parchment paper and refrigerate for at least 30 minutes to help them firm up.
3. **Coat the Crab Cakes:**
    - Place some breadcrumbs on a plate.
    - Carefully coat each crab cake in breadcrumbs, pressing gently to adhere. This helps create a crispy exterior when frying.
4. **Fry the Crab Cakes:**
    - In a large skillet, heat the vegetable oil over medium-high heat.
    - Carefully add the crab cakes to the skillet (in batches if necessary to avoid overcrowding).
    - Fry the crab cakes for about 3-4 minutes per side, or until golden brown and heated through.
    - Transfer the cooked crab cakes to a plate lined with paper towels to drain excess oil.
5. **Serve:**
    - Serve the crab cakes hot, garnished with fresh parsley and lemon wedges on the side.

- Optionally, serve with tartar sauce, remoulade, or aioli for dipping.

Enjoy these delicious homemade crab cakes as a flavorful appetizer or main dish. They're sure to impress with their crispy exterior and tender, flavorful interior filled with sweet crab meat!

Smoked salmon crostini

Ingredients:

- Baguette or crusty bread, sliced into 1/2-inch thick rounds
- Olive oil, for brushing
- 8 oz smoked salmon, thinly sliced
- 1/2 cup cream cheese or goat cheese, softened
- 2 tbsp fresh dill, chopped
- 1 tbsp capers, drained
- 1/4 red onion, thinly sliced
- Lemon zest, for garnish (optional)
- Freshly ground black pepper, to taste

Instructions:

1. Prepare the Bread:
   - Preheat the oven to 375°F (190°C).
   - Place the baguette slices on a baking sheet.
   - Brush each slice lightly with olive oil on both sides.
2. Toast the Bread:
   - Bake the bread slices in the preheated oven for about 8-10 minutes, or until they are golden and crispy. Remove from the oven and let them cool slightly.
3. Prepare the Toppings:
   - In a small bowl, mix the softened cream cheese or goat cheese with chopped fresh dill until well combined.
4. Assemble the Crostini:
   - Spread a thin layer of the cream cheese or goat cheese mixture onto each toasted baguette slice.
   - Top each crostini with a slice of smoked salmon.
   - Garnish with a few capers, thinly sliced red onion, and a sprinkle of lemon zest (if using).
   - Season with freshly ground black pepper to taste.
5. Serve:
   - Arrange the smoked salmon crostini on a serving platter.
   - Serve immediately and enjoy as a delicious and elegant appetizer.

These smoked salmon crostini are not only beautiful to look at but also bursting with flavor from the creamy cheese, savory smoked salmon, and tangy capers. They're sure to impress your guests at any gathering!

Mini pizza bites

Ingredients:

- 1 package (about 12 oz) refrigerated pizza dough
- 1/2 cup pizza sauce or marinara sauce
- 1 cup shredded mozzarella cheese
- Your choice of toppings: diced bell peppers, sliced olives, sliced pepperoni, cooked sausage, chopped mushrooms, etc.
- Fresh basil leaves, chopped (optional)
- Olive oil, for brushing
- Salt and pepper, to taste

Instructions:

1. Preheat the Oven:
   - Preheat your oven to 400°F (200°C). Line a baking sheet with parchment paper or lightly grease it.
2. Prepare the Pizza Dough:
   - Roll out the pizza dough on a lightly floured surface into a rectangle or square, about 1/4 inch thick.
   - Using a knife or pizza cutter, cut the dough into small squares or rectangles, each about 2 inches in size.
3. Assemble the Mini Pizza Bites:
   - Place the dough squares on the prepared baking sheet.
   - Spoon a small amount of pizza sauce or marinara sauce onto each dough square, spreading it out evenly.
   - Sprinkle shredded mozzarella cheese over the sauce.
   - Add your choice of toppings (bell peppers, olives, pepperoni, sausage, mushrooms, etc.) on top of the cheese.
   - Season with salt and pepper to taste.
   - Optionally, drizzle a little olive oil over the toppings for extra flavor.
4. Bake the Pizza Bites:
   - Bake in the preheated oven for 10-12 minutes, or until the cheese is melted and bubbly, and the edges of the dough are golden brown.
5. Serve:
   - Remove from the oven and let the mini pizza bites cool slightly on the baking sheet.
   - Garnish with chopped fresh basil leaves, if desired.
   - Serve warm as a delicious appetizer or snack.

These mini pizza bites are perfect for parties, game day gatherings, or even as a quick and easy weeknight dinner. They're customizable, easy to make, and sure to be a hit with everyone!

Cheese-stuffed jalapenos

Ingredients:

- 12 jalapeno peppers
- 8 oz cream cheese, softened
- 1 cup shredded cheddar cheese (or any melting cheese of your choice)
- 1/2 tsp garlic powder
- 1/2 tsp onion powder
- 1/4 tsp paprika
- Salt and pepper, to taste
- 1/2 cup breadcrumbs
- 1/4 cup grated Parmesan cheese
- Cooking spray or olive oil

Instructions:

1. Prepare the Jalapenos:
    - Preheat your oven to 375°F (190°C).
    - Cut the jalapeno peppers in half lengthwise. Use a spoon to scoop out the seeds and membranes, creating little jalapeno boats.
2. Make the Filling:
    - In a mixing bowl, combine the softened cream cheese, shredded cheddar cheese, garlic powder, onion powder, paprika, salt, and pepper. Mix until well combined.
3. Stuff the Jalapenos:
    - Spoon the cheese mixture into each jalapeno half, filling them evenly.
4. Coat the Jalapenos:
    - In a shallow dish, combine the breadcrumbs and grated Parmesan cheese.
    - Dip each stuffed jalapeno half into the breadcrumb mixture, pressing gently to coat both sides.
5. Bake the Jalapeno Poppers:
    - Place the stuffed jalapenos on a baking sheet lined with parchment paper or lightly greased.
    - Lightly spray the tops of the jalapenos with cooking spray or drizzle with a little olive oil.
    - Bake in the preheated oven for 20-25 minutes, or until the jalapenos are tender and the cheese is melted and bubbly.
6. Serve:
    - Remove from the oven and let the jalapeno poppers cool slightly before serving.
    - Enjoy these delicious cheese-stuffed jalapenos as a spicy and creamy appetizer or snack.

These cheese-stuffed jalapenos are sure to be a hit at your next gathering. They can be adjusted in spice level by removing some or all of the jalapeno seeds and membranes. Serve them with ranch dressing, salsa, or sour cream for dipping, and watch them disappear!

Chicken quesadillas

Ingredients:

- 2 cups cooked chicken, shredded or diced
- 1 cup shredded cheese (cheddar, Monterey Jack, or a blend)
- 1/2 cup diced bell peppers (any color)
- 1/4 cup diced red onion
- 1/4 cup chopped fresh cilantro
- 1 tsp ground cumin
- 1/2 tsp chili powder (optional)
- Salt and pepper, to taste
- 4 large flour tortillas
- Cooking spray or vegetable oil

Optional Garnishes:

- Sour cream
- Salsa
- Guacamole
- Chopped fresh tomatoes
- Chopped green onions

Instructions:

1. Prepare the Filling:
   - In a large bowl, combine the cooked chicken, shredded cheese, diced bell peppers, red onion, chopped cilantro, ground cumin, chili powder (if using), salt, and pepper. Mix well to combine.
2. Assemble the Quesadillas:
   - Lay out one tortilla on a flat surface.
   - Spread an even layer of the chicken and cheese mixture over half of the tortilla, leaving a small border around the edges.
   - Fold the tortilla in half to cover the filling, pressing down gently.
3. Cook the Quesadillas:
   - Heat a large skillet or griddle over medium heat.
   - Lightly spray the skillet with cooking spray or brush with a little vegetable oil.
   - Carefully place the quesadilla in the skillet and cook for 3-4 minutes on each side, or until the tortilla is golden brown and the cheese is melted.
4. Repeat:
   - Repeat the process with the remaining tortillas and filling ingredients, adjusting the heat as needed to prevent burning.
5. Serve:

- Remove the quesadillas from the skillet and let them cool for a minute before slicing.
- Slice each quesadilla into wedges.
- Serve hot with optional garnishes such as sour cream, salsa, guacamole, chopped tomatoes, and green onions.

Enjoy these delicious chicken quesadillas as a quick and flavorful meal for lunch, dinner, or even as a snack. They're versatile, customizable with your favorite ingredients, and sure to satisfy your craving for Mexican-inspired comfort food!

Fried calamari

Ingredients:

- 1 lb cleaned squid tubes and tentacles, cut into rings or strips
- 1 cup buttermilk (or regular milk)
- 1 cup all-purpose flour
- 1/2 cup cornmeal (optional, for extra crunch)
- 1 tsp salt
- 1/2 tsp black pepper
- 1/2 tsp paprika
- Vegetable oil, for frying
- Lemon wedges, for serving
- Marinara sauce or aioli, for dipping

Instructions:

1. Prepare the Calamari:
    - If not already done, clean the squid tubes and tentacles. Pat them dry with paper towels.
    - Cut the squid tubes into rings or strips, about 1/2 inch wide.
2. Marinate the Calamari:
    - Place the calamari rings and tentacles in a bowl and pour buttermilk (or regular milk) over them. Let them soak for about 15-30 minutes. This helps tenderize the calamari and adds flavor.
3. Prepare the Coating:
    - In a shallow dish, combine the all-purpose flour, cornmeal (if using), salt, black pepper, and paprika. Mix well.
4. Coat the Calamari:
    - Heat vegetable oil in a large, heavy-bottomed pot or deep fryer to 350°F (175°C).
    - Remove the calamari from the buttermilk, allowing excess to drip off.
    - Dredge the calamari rings and tentacles in the flour mixture, coating them evenly. Shake off any excess flour.
5. Fry the Calamari:
    - Carefully drop a few pieces of calamari into the hot oil, making sure not to overcrowd the pot. Fry in batches if necessary.
    - Fry for 1-2 minutes, or until the calamari is golden brown and crispy. Be careful not to overcook, as calamari can become tough.
6. Drain and Serve:
    - Use a slotted spoon or tongs to remove the fried calamari from the oil. Place them on a plate lined with paper towels to drain excess oil.
    - Sprinkle with a little extra salt while still hot, if desired.
    - Serve immediately with lemon wedges and marinara sauce or aioli for dipping.

Enjoy your homemade crispy fried calamari as a delightful appetizer or part of a seafood meal. It's a dish that's sure to impress with its crunchy texture and delicate flavor!

Poutine

Ingredients:

- 4 cups frozen french fries (or homemade if preferred)
- 1 1/2 cups cheese curds (cheddar cheese curds are traditional, but any cheese curds will work)
- 2 cups beef gravy (homemade or store-bought)

Instructions:

1. Cook the French Fries:
   - Preheat your oven and cook the frozen french fries according to the package instructions, or prepare homemade french fries if preferred.
2. Prepare the Gravy:
   - While the french fries are cooking, heat the beef gravy in a saucepan over medium heat until heated through. Keep warm until ready to use.
3. Assemble the Poutine:
   - Once the french fries are cooked and still hot, divide them among serving plates or a large platter.
   - Sprinkle the cheese curds evenly over the hot french fries.
4. Pour the Gravy:
   - Ladle the hot beef gravy over the cheese curds and french fries. The heat from the fries and gravy will help melt the cheese curds.
5. Serve Immediately:
   - Serve the poutine immediately while hot, ensuring that the cheese curds are melted and gooey.
   - Optionally, garnish with chopped fresh parsley or green onions for added flavor and color.

Poutine is best enjoyed fresh and hot, with the cheese curds melting into the gravy and coating the crispy french fries. It's a hearty and indulgent dish that's perfect for sharing with friends and family, especially during cold weather or as a comforting treat!

Meatball sliders

Ingredients:

- 12 slider buns (mini hamburger buns)
- 12 cooked meatballs (homemade or store-bought, about 1-inch in diameter)
- 1 cup marinara sauce
- 1 cup shredded mozzarella cheese (or cheese of your choice)
- 2 tbsp melted butter
- 1/2 tsp garlic powder
- 1/2 tsp dried oregano
- Fresh basil or parsley, chopped (optional)
- Grated Parmesan cheese (optional)
- Salt and pepper, to taste

Instructions:

1. Preheat the Oven:
   - Preheat your oven to 350°F (175°C).
2. Prepare the Meatballs:
   - If using store-bought meatballs, follow the package instructions to cook them until heated through. If using homemade meatballs, ensure they are fully cooked.
3. Assemble the Sliders:
   - Slice the slider buns in half horizontally and place the bottom halves in a baking dish or on a baking sheet lined with parchment paper.
   - Place one meatball on each bottom half of the slider buns.
   - Spoon marinara sauce over each meatball, dividing it evenly.
   - Sprinkle shredded mozzarella cheese over the marinara sauce.
4. Cover with the Top Buns:
   - Place the top halves of the slider buns over the cheese and meatballs to form sandwiches.
5. Make the Garlic Butter Topping:
   - In a small bowl, mix together melted butter, garlic powder, dried oregano, salt, and pepper.
6. Brush the Sliders:
   - Brush the tops of the slider buns with the garlic butter mixture.
7. Bake the Sliders:
   - Cover the baking dish with foil and bake in the preheated oven for 15-20 minutes, or until the cheese is melted and the sliders are heated through.
8. Serve:
   - Remove from the oven and sprinkle with chopped fresh basil or parsley and grated Parmesan cheese if desired.
   - Serve warm and enjoy these delicious meatball sliders as a hearty appetizer or meal.

These meatball sliders are perfect for parties, game day gatherings, or even a quick and easy weeknight dinner. They're sure to be a crowd-pleaser with their flavorful meatballs, gooey cheese, and garlic butter topping!

Chicken satay with peanut sauce

Chicken Satay Ingredients:

- 1 lb boneless, skinless chicken breasts or thighs, cut into thin strips or cubes
- Bamboo skewers, soaked in water for at least 30 minutes (if using wooden skewers)
- 2 cloves garlic, minced
- 1 tbsp lemongrass, minced (optional)
- 1 tbsp soy sauce
- 1 tbsp fish sauce
- 1 tbsp brown sugar
- 1 tbsp vegetable oil
- 1/2 tsp ground coriander
- 1/2 tsp ground cumin
- 1/4 tsp turmeric powder (optional, for color)
- Salt and pepper, to taste

Peanut Sauce Ingredients:

- 1/2 cup creamy peanut butter
- 1/4 cup coconut milk (or more for desired consistency)
- 2 tbsp soy sauce
- 1 tbsp brown sugar
- 1 tbsp lime juice
- 1 clove garlic, minced
- 1/2 tsp grated fresh ginger
- 1/4 tsp red pepper flakes (optional, for heat)
- Water, as needed to thin out the sauce

Instructions:

1. Marinate the Chicken:
    - In a bowl, combine minced garlic, lemongrass (if using), soy sauce, fish sauce, brown sugar, vegetable oil, ground coriander, ground cumin, turmeric powder (if using), salt, and pepper.
    - Add the chicken strips or cubes to the marinade and toss until well-coated. Cover and refrigerate for at least 1 hour, or overnight for best flavor.
2. Make the Peanut Sauce:
    - In a small saucepan over medium-low heat, combine creamy peanut butter, coconut milk, soy sauce, brown sugar, lime juice, minced garlic, grated ginger, and red pepper flakes (if using).
    - Stir continuously until the peanut butter melts and the sauce becomes smooth and creamy. If the sauce is too thick, add water gradually until you reach your desired consistency. Remove from heat and set aside.

3. Prepare the Chicken Satay:
    - Preheat your grill or grill pan over medium-high heat.
    - Thread the marinated chicken strips or cubes onto the soaked bamboo skewers.
4. Grill the Chicken Satay:
    - Grill the chicken skewers for 3-4 minutes on each side, or until cooked through and slightly charred. Cooking time may vary depending on the thickness of the chicken pieces.
5. Serve:
    - Arrange the grilled chicken satay on a serving platter.
    - Serve with the prepared peanut sauce on the side for dipping or drizzle the sauce over the chicken skewers.
    - Garnish with chopped peanuts, cilantro, or lime wedges if desired.

Enjoy these delicious chicken satay skewers with peanut sauce as an appetizer or main dish. They are perfect for parties and gatherings, offering a wonderful blend of savory, sweet, and nutty flavors!

Stuffed bell peppers

Ingredients:

- 4 large bell peppers (any color)
- 1 lb ground beef (or ground turkey, chicken, or sausage)
- 1 cup cooked rice (white or brown)
- 1/2 cup diced onion
- 2 cloves garlic, minced
- 1 cup diced tomatoes (fresh or canned)
- 1 cup shredded cheese (cheddar, mozzarella, or your favorite melting cheese)
- 1 tbsp tomato paste
- 1 tsp dried oregano
- 1 tsp dried basil
- Salt and pepper, to taste
- Olive oil, for cooking
- Fresh parsley or basil, chopped (for garnish)

Instructions:

1. Prepare the Bell Peppers:
    - Preheat your oven to 375°F (190°C).
    - Cut the tops off the bell peppers and remove the seeds and membranes from inside. Set aside.
2. Prepare the Filling:
    - In a large skillet, heat olive oil over medium heat.
    - Add diced onion and minced garlic. Sauté until softened and fragrant, about 2-3 minutes.
3. Cook the Ground Meat:
    - Add ground beef (or your choice of ground meat) to the skillet with the onions and garlic. Cook until browned and no longer pink, breaking it up with a spoon as it cooks.
4. Add Tomatoes and Seasoning:
    - Stir in diced tomatoes, tomato paste, dried oregano, dried basil, salt, and pepper. Cook for another 2-3 minutes to combine the flavors.
5. Combine with Rice:
    - Remove the skillet from heat. Stir in cooked rice until well combined with the meat mixture. Adjust seasoning if needed.
6. Stuff the Bell Peppers:
    - Spoon the filling mixture evenly into the hollowed-out bell peppers, pressing down gently to pack the filling.
7. Bake the Stuffed Bell Peppers:
    - Place the stuffed bell peppers upright in a baking dish. Cover with foil and bake in the preheated oven for 30-35 minutes, or until the peppers are tender.

8. Add Cheese and Finish Baking:
    - Remove the foil and sprinkle shredded cheese evenly over the tops of the stuffed peppers.
    - Return to the oven and bake uncovered for an additional 10 minutes, or until the cheese is melted and bubbly.
9. Serve:
    - Remove from the oven and let the stuffed bell peppers cool slightly before serving.
    - Garnish with chopped fresh parsley or basil, if desired.

Enjoy these delicious stuffed bell peppers as a nutritious and satisfying meal. They are great for dinner and can be prepared ahead of time for easy reheating later!

Buffalo cauliflower bites

Ingredients:

- 1 head of cauliflower, cut into florets
- 1 cup all-purpose flour
- 1 cup milk (or plant-based milk for vegan option)
- 1 tsp garlic powder
- 1 tsp onion powder
- 1/2 tsp paprika
- Salt and pepper, to taste
- 1 cup buffalo sauce (store-bought or homemade)
- 2 tbsp unsalted butter (or vegan butter)
- Ranch or blue cheese dressing, for dipping (optional)
- Celery sticks, for serving (optional)

Instructions:

1. Prepare the Cauliflower:
   - Preheat your oven to 450°F (230°C).
   - Line a baking sheet with parchment paper or lightly grease it.
2. Prepare the Batter:
   - In a large bowl, whisk together flour, milk, garlic powder, onion powder, paprika, salt, and pepper until smooth and well combined.
3. Coat the Cauliflower:
   - Dip each cauliflower floret into the batter, shaking off any excess, and place them on the prepared baking sheet in a single layer.
4. Bake the Cauliflower:
   - Bake in the preheated oven for 20-25 minutes, or until the cauliflower is golden brown and crispy. Flip halfway through baking for even cooking.
5. Make the Buffalo Sauce:
   - While the cauliflower is baking, melt butter in a small saucepan over medium heat.
   - Stir in buffalo sauce and cook for 1-2 minutes, stirring occasionally. Remove from heat.
6. Coat the Cauliflower with Buffalo Sauce:
   - Once the cauliflower is done baking, transfer the florets to a large bowl.
   - Pour the buffalo sauce mixture over the cauliflower and toss gently to coat evenly.
7. Serve:
   - Arrange the buffalo cauliflower bites on a serving platter.
   - Serve with ranch or blue cheese dressing and celery sticks on the side for dipping.

Enjoy these crispy and flavorful buffalo cauliflower bites as a delicious appetizer or snack, perfect for game day or any gathering. They are a great vegetarian or vegan option that satisfies cravings for spicy buffalo flavors!

Shrimp cocktail

Ingredients:

- 1 lb large shrimp, peeled and deveined (tails left on, optional)
- 1 lemon, halved
- Ice, for serving

For the Cocktail Sauce:

- 1/2 cup ketchup
- 2 tbsp prepared horseradish (adjust to taste)
- 1 tbsp fresh lemon juice
- 1 tsp Worcestershire sauce
- 1/2 tsp hot sauce (optional, adjust to taste)
- Salt and pepper, to taste

Instructions:

1. Cook the Shrimp:
    - Fill a large pot with water and add a generous pinch of salt.
    - Squeeze the juice from one half of the lemon into the water and add the lemon half itself.
    - Bring the water to a boil over high heat.
    - Add the shrimp to the boiling water and cook for 2-3 minutes, or until the shrimp are pink and opaque. Be careful not to overcook.
    - Drain the shrimp immediately and transfer them to a bowl of ice water to stop the cooking process.
    - Once cooled, drain the shrimp and refrigerate until ready to serve.
2. Prepare the Cocktail Sauce:
    - In a small bowl, mix together ketchup, prepared horseradish, fresh lemon juice, Worcestershire sauce, hot sauce (if using), salt, and pepper.
    - Adjust seasoning to taste, adding more horseradish or hot sauce for extra heat if desired.
    - Cover and refrigerate the cocktail sauce until ready to serve.
3. Assemble and Serve:
    - Arrange the chilled shrimp on a serving platter or individual cocktail glasses.
    - Serve the shrimp with the cocktail sauce in a bowl or ramekin on the side.
    - Garnish with lemon wedges and fresh parsley or dill, if desired.
4. Enjoy:
    - Serve the shrimp cocktail immediately as a refreshing appetizer.

Shrimp cocktail is best served chilled and can be prepared ahead of time, making it a convenient choice for parties and gatherings. It's light, flavorful, and sure to impress your guests!

Teriyaki meatballs

Ingredients:

For the Meatballs:

- 1 lb ground beef (or ground chicken, turkey, pork)
- 1/2 cup breadcrumbs
- 1/4 cup milk
- 1 egg
- 2 cloves garlic, minced
- 2 green onions, finely chopped
- 1 tbsp soy sauce
- Salt and pepper, to taste
- 1 tbsp vegetable oil (for cooking)

For the Teriyaki Sauce:

- 1/2 cup soy sauce
- 1/4 cup water
- 1/4 cup brown sugar (or honey)
- 2 tbsp rice vinegar (or apple cider vinegar)
- 1 clove garlic, minced
- 1 tsp grated fresh ginger (or 1/2 tsp ground ginger)
- 1 tbsp cornstarch mixed with 2 tbsp water (optional, for thickening)

Instructions:

1. Make the Meatballs:
    - Preheat your oven to 400°F (200°C).
    - In a large bowl, combine ground meat, breadcrumbs, milk, egg, minced garlic, chopped green onions, soy sauce, salt, and pepper. Mix until well combined.
    - Shape the mixture into meatballs, about 1 inch in diameter.
2. Cook the Meatballs:
    - Heat vegetable oil in a large skillet over medium-high heat.
    - Add the meatballs in batches, cooking until browned on all sides, about 5-7 minutes. Transfer cooked meatballs to a plate lined with paper towels to drain excess oil.
3. Make the Teriyaki Sauce:
    - In the same skillet, combine soy sauce, water, brown sugar (or honey), rice vinegar, minced garlic, and grated ginger. Bring to a simmer over medium heat.
    - If you want a thicker sauce, stir in the cornstarch mixture (cornstarch mixed with water). Cook, stirring constantly, until the sauce thickens to your desired consistency.
4. Combine Meatballs and Sauce:

- Add the cooked meatballs back into the skillet with the teriyaki sauce.
- Toss the meatballs gently in the sauce until evenly coated. Simmer for another 2-3 minutes to heat through.
5. Serve:
    - Serve the teriyaki meatballs hot, garnished with sliced green onions or sesame seeds if desired.
    - They can be served as appetizers with toothpicks or as a main dish over rice or noodles.

Enjoy these flavorful teriyaki meatballs as a delicious and satisfying meal!

Sweet potato fries

Ingredients:

- 2 large sweet potatoes
- 2 tbsp olive oil
- 1 tsp paprika (optional, for extra flavor)
- 1/2 tsp garlic powder
- 1/2 tsp onion powder
- Salt and pepper, to taste
- Fresh parsley or cilantro, chopped (optional, for garnish)

Instructions:

1. Preheat the Oven:
    - Preheat your oven to 425°F (220°C). Line a baking sheet with parchment paper or aluminum foil for easy cleanup.
2. Prepare the Sweet Potatoes:
    - Wash and peel the sweet potatoes.
    - Cut the sweet potatoes into even-sized fries, about 1/4 to 1/2 inch thick. Try to keep them as uniform as possible for even cooking.
3. Season the Fries:
    - In a large bowl, toss the sweet potato fries with olive oil, paprika (if using), garlic powder, onion powder, salt, and pepper. Mix well until the fries are evenly coated with the seasoning.
4. Arrange on Baking Sheet:
    - Spread the seasoned sweet potato fries in a single layer on the prepared baking sheet. Make sure they are not overlapping to ensure they crisp up evenly.
5. Bake the Fries:
    - Bake in the preheated oven for 20-25 minutes, flipping halfway through with a spatula. Bake until the fries are golden brown and crispy on the outside.
6. Serve:
    - Remove from the oven and let the sweet potato fries cool slightly on the baking sheet.
    - Transfer to a serving plate and garnish with chopped fresh parsley or cilantro if desired.
    - Serve hot with your favorite dipping sauce, such as ketchup, aioli, or ranch dressing.

Enjoy these crispy and flavorful sweet potato fries as a tasty side dish or snack. They are perfect for serving alongside burgers, sandwiches, or as a healthier alternative to regular fries!

Cucumber rolls with cream cheese

Ingredients:

- 1 large cucumber
- 4 oz cream cheese, softened
- 1 tbsp fresh dill, chopped (or 1 tsp dried dill)
- 1 tbsp fresh chives, chopped (optional)
- Salt and pepper, to taste
- Thinly sliced smoked salmon or deli meat (optional, for variation)

Instructions:

1. Prepare the Cucumber:
    - Wash the cucumber thoroughly. If desired, peel strips of the cucumber skin lengthwise to create a striped effect.
2. Slice the Cucumber:
    - Using a vegetable peeler or a mandoline slicer, slice the cucumber lengthwise into thin, long strips. Aim for slices that are about 1/8 inch thick.
3. Make the Cream Cheese Filling:
    - In a small bowl, mix together the softened cream cheese, chopped fresh dill, chopped chives (if using), salt, and pepper. Stir until well combined and smooth.
4. Assemble the Cucumber Rolls:
    - Lay out a cucumber slice on a clean work surface.
    - Spread a thin layer of the cream cheese mixture evenly over the cucumber slice, leaving a small border around the edges.
    - Optionally, place a slice of smoked salmon or deli meat on top of the cream cheese layer, if using.
5. Roll Up the Cucumber:
    - Carefully roll up the cucumber slice, starting from one end and rolling towards the other end. The cream cheese filling should hold the roll together.
6. Repeat:
    - Repeat the process with the remaining cucumber slices and cream cheese mixture until all slices are used.
7. Chill and Serve:
    - Arrange the cucumber rolls on a serving platter.
    - If desired, chill in the refrigerator for about 15-30 minutes to firm up before serving.
    - Garnish with additional fresh dill or chives, if desired.
8. Serve:
    - Serve the cucumber rolls with cream cheese as a refreshing appetizer or snack.

These cucumber rolls with cream cheese are light, refreshing, and customizable. They make a perfect addition to any party platter or a light lunch option. Enjoy experimenting with different fillings and garnishes to suit your taste!

BBQ chicken drumsticks

Ingredients:

- 8 chicken drumsticks
- 1 cup BBQ sauce (store-bought or homemade)
- 2 tbsp olive oil
- 1 tbsp paprika
- 1 tbsp garlic powder
- 1 tbsp onion powder
- 1 tsp salt
- 1/2 tsp black pepper
- Fresh parsley or cilantro, chopped (optional, for garnish)

Instructions:

1. Marinate the Chicken:
   - In a large bowl, combine olive oil, paprika, garlic powder, onion powder, salt, and black pepper. Mix well to create a marinade.
   - Add the chicken drumsticks to the marinade, ensuring they are evenly coated. Cover the bowl with plastic wrap or transfer to a resealable plastic bag. Marinate in the refrigerator for at least 1 hour, or overnight for best flavor.
2. Preheat the Grill or Oven:
   - If grilling, preheat your grill to medium-high heat (about 375-400°F / 190-200°C). If baking, preheat your oven to 400°F (200°C).
3. Grill or Bake the Chicken:
   - If grilling: Remove the chicken drumsticks from the marinade and place them on the preheated grill. Cook for about 20-25 minutes, turning occasionally, until the chicken is cooked through and reaches an internal temperature of 165°F (74°C). Brush with BBQ sauce during the last 5-10 minutes of cooking, turning and brushing with sauce until caramelized and sticky.
   - If baking: Place the marinated chicken drumsticks on a baking sheet lined with aluminum foil or parchment paper. Bake in the preheated oven for 35-40 minutes, turning once halfway through cooking. Brush with BBQ sauce during the last 10-15 minutes of baking, turning and brushing with sauce until caramelized and sticky.
4. Serve:
   - Transfer the BBQ chicken drumsticks to a serving platter.
   - Garnish with chopped fresh parsley or cilantro, if desired.
   - Serve hot with extra BBQ sauce on the side for dipping.

Enjoy these BBQ chicken drumsticks as a delicious main dish for a casual dinner or as a crowd-pleasing option for a barbecue or party. They're juicy, flavorful, and perfect for summer grilling!

Bruschetta with tomato and basil

Ingredients:

- 4-6 slices of Italian bread (baguette works well)
- 2-3 ripe tomatoes, diced
- 1-2 cloves garlic, minced
- 6-8 fresh basil leaves, thinly sliced (chiffonade)
- 2 tbsp extra virgin olive oil
- 1 tbsp balsamic vinegar (optional)
- Salt and pepper, to taste

Instructions:

1. Prepare the Bread:
    - Preheat your oven to 400°F (200°C).
    - Place the bread slices on a baking sheet and brush both sides lightly with olive oil. You can also grill the bread on a grill pan for added flavor.
2. Toast the Bread:
    - Bake the bread slices in the preheated oven for about 5-7 minutes, or until they are golden brown and crispy. Alternatively, grill the bread slices on a grill pan until they have grill marks on both sides.
3. Prepare the Tomato Basil Topping:
    - In a mixing bowl, combine diced tomatoes, minced garlic, sliced basil, olive oil, and balsamic vinegar (if using).
    - Season with salt and pepper to taste. Mix well to combine all the flavors.
4. Assemble the Bruschetta:
    - Remove the toasted bread slices from the oven or grill and place them on a serving platter.
    - Spoon the tomato basil mixture generously over each slice of bread, ensuring the toppings are evenly distributed.
5. Serve:
    - Garnish the bruschetta with additional basil leaves for decoration, if desired.
    - Serve immediately as an appetizer or light snack.

Bruschetta with tomato and basil is best enjoyed fresh, allowing the flavors of the tomatoes, garlic, and basil to shine. It's a perfect dish for summer gatherings, using seasonal ingredients for a burst of Mediterranean flavors!

Bacon-wrapped scallops

Ingredients:

- Fresh scallops (large, about 12-16 pieces)
- Thinly sliced bacon (12-16 slices, depending on the number of scallops)
- Olive oil
- Salt and pepper
- Toothpicks or skewers (if needed)

Instructions:

1. Prepare the scallops:
    - If using frozen scallops, thaw them completely and pat them dry with paper towels. It's important to remove excess moisture to ensure the bacon crisps up properly.
2. Prepare the bacon:
    - Precook the bacon slightly to render some of the fat. You can do this by placing the bacon slices on a microwave-safe plate lined with paper towels and microwaving for about 1-2 minutes until partially cooked but still pliable. This step helps the bacon crisp up more evenly during baking.
3. Wrap the scallops:
    - Preheat your oven to 400°F (200°C).
    - Take each scallop and wrap it with a slice of partially cooked bacon. Secure the bacon with a toothpick or small skewer to hold it in place. Place each wrapped scallop on a baking sheet lined with parchment paper or aluminum foil.
4. Season:
    - Lightly brush each bacon-wrapped scallop with olive oil and season with salt and pepper to taste.
5. Bake:
    - Bake in the preheated oven for about 15-20 minutes, or until the bacon is crispy and the scallops are cooked through. The internal temperature of the scallops should reach 120°F (49°C) to be fully cooked.
6. Serve:
    - Once done, remove from the oven and let them cool slightly. Remove the toothpicks or skewers before serving.

Serving Suggestions:

- You can serve bacon-wrapped scallops as an appetizer with a dipping sauce like garlic aioli or a tangy cocktail sauce.
- As a main dish, consider serving them over a bed of rice or alongside a fresh salad.

Enjoy your bacon-wrapped scallops! They make a delightful dish for any occasion, combining the flavors of the sea and the savory goodness of bacon.

Cornbread muffins

Ingredients:

- 1 cup yellow cornmeal
- 1 cup all-purpose flour
- 1/4 cup granulated sugar (adjust to taste)
- 1 tablespoon baking powder
- 1/2 teaspoon baking soda
- 1/2 teaspoon salt
- 1 cup buttermilk (or substitute with 1 cup milk + 1 tablespoon vinegar or lemon juice, let sit for 5 minutes)
- 1/2 cup unsalted butter, melted and cooled slightly
- 2 large eggs

Optional add-ins:

- 1/2 cup shredded cheddar cheese
- 1/4 cup chopped green onions
- 1/4 cup diced jalapeños (for a spicy kick)

Instructions:

1. Preheat oven and prepare muffin tin:
   - Preheat your oven to 400°F (200°C). Grease a 12-cup muffin tin or line with paper liners.
2. Mix dry ingredients:
   - In a large bowl, whisk together the cornmeal, flour, sugar, baking powder, baking soda, and salt until well combined.
3. Mix wet ingredients:
   - In another bowl, whisk together the buttermilk, melted butter, and eggs until well combined.
4. Combine wet and dry ingredients:
   - Pour the wet ingredients into the dry ingredients and stir until just combined. Do not overmix; it's okay if the batter is slightly lumpy. If adding any optional ingredients like cheese, green onions, or jalapeños, fold them in gently at this stage.
5. Fill muffin tin:
   - Spoon the batter into the prepared muffin tin, filling each cup about 3/4 full.
6. Bake:
   - Bake in the preheated oven for 15-18 minutes, or until the tops are golden brown and a toothpick inserted into the center of a muffin comes out clean.
7. Cool and serve:

- Remove the muffins from the tin and let them cool on a wire rack for a few minutes before serving.

Serving Suggestions:

- Serve cornbread muffins warm with a pat of butter and a drizzle of honey.
- Pair them with chili, soups, stews, or BBQ dishes for a comforting meal.
- They also make a great addition to brunch or as a snack on their own.

Enjoy these homemade cornbread muffins, which are moist, slightly sweet, and perfect for any occasion!

Stuffed jalapeno poppers

Ingredients:

- 12 jalapeno peppers
- 8 oz cream cheese, softened
- 1 cup shredded cheddar cheese (or cheese of your choice)
- 1/2 teaspoon garlic powder
- 1/2 teaspoon onion powder
- Salt and pepper, to taste
- 12 slices of bacon, cut in half (optional for wrapping)

Instructions:

1. Prepare the jalapenos:
    - Preheat your oven to 400°F (200°C). Line a baking sheet with parchment paper.
2. Prepare the peppers:
    - Wash the jalapeno peppers thoroughly. Cut each pepper in half lengthwise and carefully remove the seeds and membranes. Wear gloves or wash your hands thoroughly after handling the jalapenos, especially if you are sensitive to spicy foods.
3. Make the filling:
    - In a mixing bowl, combine the softened cream cheese, shredded cheddar cheese, garlic powder, onion powder, salt, and pepper. Mix until well combined and smooth.
4. Stuff the peppers:
    - Spoon the cheese mixture evenly into each jalapeno half, filling them until slightly mounded.
5. Wrap with bacon (optional):
    - If desired, wrap each stuffed jalapeno half with a half-slice of bacon. Secure the bacon with a toothpick if needed.
6. Bake the poppers:
    - Place the stuffed jalapeno halves on the prepared baking sheet. Bake in the preheated oven for 20-25 minutes, or until the peppers are softened, the cheese is melted and bubbly, and the bacon is crispy.
7. Serve:
    - Remove from the oven and let cool for a few minutes before serving. Serve the stuffed jalapeno poppers warm as a delicious appetizer or party snack.

Serving Suggestions:

- Serve with ranch dressing, sour cream, or salsa for dipping.
- These poppers are great for parties, game nights, or as a side dish for barbecues.

Enjoy these stuffed jalapeno poppers with their creamy, cheesy filling and crispy bacon (if added), offering a delightful combination of flavors and textures!

Philly cheesesteak sliders

Ingredients:

- 1 lb thinly sliced steak (such as ribeye or sirloin)
- 1 onion, thinly sliced
- 1 green bell pepper, thinly sliced
- 12 slider buns (or small dinner rolls)
- 8 oz provolone cheese, sliced or shredded
- 2 tablespoons olive oil
- Salt and pepper, to taste
- Optional: garlic powder, Worcestershire sauce, hot sauce

Instructions:

1. Prepare the ingredients:
   - Preheat your oven to 350°F (175°C).
   - Thinly slice the steak against the grain. Season with salt, pepper, and any optional seasonings like garlic powder or a splash of Worcestershire sauce.
2. Cook the steak and vegetables:
   - In a large skillet, heat 1 tablespoon of olive oil over medium-high heat. Add the thinly sliced steak and cook until browned and cooked through, about 3-4 minutes per side. Remove the steak from the skillet and set aside.
   - In the same skillet, add another tablespoon of olive oil if needed. Add the thinly sliced onions and bell peppers. Cook, stirring occasionally, until the vegetables are softened and lightly caramelized, about 5-7 minutes. Season with salt and pepper to taste.
3. Assemble the sliders:
   - Slice the slider buns in half horizontally and place the bottom halves on a baking sheet.
   - Layer the cooked steak evenly over the bottom halves of the slider buns.
   - Top the steak with the cooked onions and bell peppers.
4. Add cheese:
   - Place slices or sprinkle shredded provolone cheese evenly over the onions and bell peppers.
5. Bake:
   - Cover the sliders with the top halves of the buns. Bake in the preheated oven for about 10 minutes, or until the cheese is melted and the sliders are heated through.
6. Serve:
   - Remove from the oven and serve immediately. Optionally, you can brush the tops of the sliders with melted butter and sprinkle with sesame seeds before baking for added flavor and texture.

Serving Suggestions:

- Serve Philly cheesesteak sliders hot, straight from the oven.
- Offer condiments like ketchup, mayo, or hot sauce on the side for dipping or drizzling.
- These sliders pair well with a side of coleslaw, potato chips, or a green salad.

Enjoy these Philly cheesesteak sliders as a tasty and satisfying dish that's sure to be a hit at any gathering!

Mediterranean platter with hummus and pita

Ingredients:

- Hummus:
  - Store-bought or homemade hummus (you can find recipes for homemade hummus easily online).
- Pita Bread:
  - 4-6 pieces of pita bread, cut into triangles or wedges.
- Olives:
  - A variety of olives such as Kalamata, green, or stuffed olives.
- Cheese:
  - Feta cheese, sliced or crumbled.
- Vegetables:
  - Cherry tomatoes, cucumber slices, carrot sticks, bell pepper strips, or any other fresh vegetables of your choice.
- Dips and Spreads:
  - Tzatziki sauce (yogurt and cucumber dip), baba ganoush (roasted eggplant dip), or any other Mediterranean dips you enjoy.
- Extras:
  - Fresh herbs like parsley or dill for garnish.
  - Lemon wedges for squeezing over the vegetables.

Assembly:

1. Prepare the Hummus and Pita:
   - If making homemade hummus, prepare it according to your chosen recipe. Otherwise, transfer store-bought hummus into a serving bowl.
2. Prepare the Pita Bread:
   - Cut the pita bread into triangles or wedges. You can lightly toast them in the oven or serve them as is.
3. Arrange on a Platter:
   - Place the bowl of hummus in the center of a large platter or serving board.
   - Arrange the pita bread triangles around the hummus bowl.
   - Place the olives, feta cheese, and vegetables in small piles or groups around the platter, creating an aesthetically pleasing arrangement.
4. Add Dips and Spreads:
   - If serving additional dips like tzatziki or baba ganoush, place them in small bowls on the platter.
5. Garnish and Serve:
   - Garnish the platter with fresh herbs, like parsley or dill, for added color and flavor.
   - Serve the Mediterranean platter with lemon wedges on the side for squeezing over the vegetables.

Serving Suggestions:

- Mediterranean platters are great for parties, gatherings, or as a light lunch or dinner option.
- Serve with additional warm pita bread or crackers if desired.
- Pair with a glass of chilled white wine or a refreshing lemonade.

Enjoy assembling and serving this Mediterranean platter with hummus and pita, showcasing the vibrant flavors and freshness of Mediterranean cuisine!

Asian chicken wings

Ingredients:

- 2 lbs chicken wings, separated into flats and drumettes
- 1/4 cup soy sauce
- 1/4 cup hoisin sauce
- 2 tablespoons honey
- 2 tablespoons rice vinegar
- 2 cloves garlic, minced
- 1 tablespoon grated fresh ginger
- 1 teaspoon sesame oil
- 1 tablespoon sriracha sauce (adjust to taste)
- Salt and pepper, to taste
- Sesame seeds and chopped green onions, for garnish

Instructions:

1. Marinate the chicken wings:
    - In a large bowl or resealable plastic bag, combine soy sauce, hoisin sauce, honey, rice vinegar, minced garlic, grated ginger, sesame oil, sriracha sauce, salt, and pepper. Mix well to combine.
    - Add the chicken wings to the marinade and toss until evenly coated. Marinate in the refrigerator for at least 1 hour, or overnight for best results.
2. Preheat the oven:
    - Preheat your oven to 400°F (200°C). Line a baking sheet with parchment paper or aluminum foil and place a wire rack on top.
3. Arrange the chicken wings:
    - Remove the chicken wings from the marinade and shake off excess marinade. Place the wings in a single layer on the wire rack, leaving space between each wing.
4. Bake the wings:
    - Bake in the preheated oven for 40-45 minutes, turning halfway through, or until the wings are cooked through and crispy.
5. Optional: Broil for crispiness (if desired):
    - If you prefer extra crispy wings, you can broil them for an additional 2-3 minutes after baking, keeping a close eye to prevent burning.
6. Garnish and serve:
    - Remove the wings from the oven and transfer them to a serving platter. Sprinkle with sesame seeds and chopped green onions for garnish.
7. Serve with dipping sauce (optional):
    - Serve the Asian chicken wings hot, with additional sriracha mayo, sweet chili sauce, or soy sauce on the side for dipping.

Serving Suggestions:

- Asian chicken wings are perfect as an appetizer for parties or as a main dish served with rice and steamed vegetables.
- Pair with a refreshing Asian-inspired salad dressed with sesame ginger dressing.
- Enjoy with an ice-cold beer or a glass of chilled sake for a complete Asian dining experience.

These Asian chicken wings are sure to be a hit with their savory, sweet, and slightly spicy flavors, making them a crowd-pleasing dish for any occasion!

Chocolate-covered strawberries

Ingredients:

- Fresh strawberries (about 1 pound or 454 grams)
- 8 ounces (about 225 grams) of high-quality semi-sweet or dark chocolate
- Optional: White chocolate, for drizzling
- Optional: Chopped nuts, shredded coconut, sprinkles, or other toppings for decoration

Instructions:

1. Prepare the strawberries:
    - Wash the strawberries thoroughly and pat them completely dry with paper towels. It's important for the strawberries to be completely dry to ensure the chocolate adheres well.
2. Melt the chocolate:
    - Chop the chocolate into small pieces and place them in a microwave-safe bowl or a heatproof bowl set over a pot of simmering water (double boiler method). If using the microwave, heat the chocolate in short 20-30 second bursts, stirring well between each interval until melted and smooth.
3. Dip the strawberries:
    - Hold each strawberry by the stem (or use a toothpick inserted into the stem end) and dip it into the melted chocolate, swirling to coat evenly. Allow any excess chocolate to drip back into the bowl.
4. Place on parchment paper:
    - Place the chocolate-covered strawberry onto a baking sheet lined with parchment paper. Repeat with the remaining strawberries.
5. Optional: Decorate with toppings:
    - While the chocolate is still wet, sprinkle the strawberries with chopped nuts, shredded coconut, sprinkles, or any other toppings you desire. This step adds extra flavor and texture to your chocolate-covered strawberries.
6. Let the chocolate set:
    - Allow the chocolate-covered strawberries to sit at room temperature until the chocolate sets, or place them in the refrigerator for about 15-30 minutes to speed up the process.
7. Optional: Drizzle with white chocolate:
    - Melt white chocolate using the same method as for the dark chocolate. Drizzle the melted white chocolate over the chocolate-covered strawberries for an elegant decorative touch.
8. Serve and enjoy:
    - Once the chocolate is completely set, arrange the chocolate-covered strawberries on a serving platter or plate. They are best enjoyed fresh but can be stored in the refrigerator for up to 24 hours. Bring them to room temperature before serving for the best texture.

Tips:

- Use high-quality chocolate for the best flavor and smooth texture.
- Customize your chocolate-covered strawberries with different types of chocolate, toppings, or even a touch of sea salt for a gourmet twist.
- If making ahead, store the strawberries in a single layer in an airtight container in the refrigerator. Bring them to room temperature before serving.

These chocolate-covered strawberries make a delightful treat for special occasions, romantic dinners, or any time you want to indulge in something sweet and decadent!

www.ingramcontent.com/pod-product-compliance
Lightning Source LLC
LaVergne TN
LVHW061946070526
838199LV00060B/4002